# Broadfork Farm

*Trout Lake, Washington*

# Broadfork Farm

*Trout Lake, Washington*

Poems by Tricia Knoll

A Publication of The Poetry Box®

Library of Congress Control Number: 2017944622

ISBN-13:  978-0-9980999-4-1
ISBN-10:  0-9980999-4-5

Published by The Poetry Box®, 2017
Beaverton, Oregon
www.ThePoetryBox.com
530.409.0721

# Dedication

Deep thanks to the family who lives at Broadfork Farm — Kaye Jones, Adam Hyde, Rye Jones-Hyde, Fisher Jones-Hyde and Archer Jones-Hyde — for trusting us as farmsitters.

Much love to the animals including Bear, Willa, Trout, Mary, Lucia and the many others we have cared for.

Thanks too to my daughter Gillian Galford Trevithick for keeping the friendship alive with this family and the farm's wonderful beings, and for marrying Dave Trevithick at Broadfork Farm on July 25, 2015.

To my husband Darrell Salk who has fixed how the front gate swings, worked to make sure all beings had water when a hydrant valve failed, and who joins me to farmsit and take photos.

# Table of Contents

# Introduction

## Broadfork Farm in Trout Lake, Washington

Trout Lake doesn't show up on every Washington map. This small town (557 people in the recent census) in Klickitat County is home to four dairies and an organic farm that grows more than two-dozen herbs and botanicals. Cascadia Creamery ages artisanal organic raw-milk cheeses in lava tube caves. The town is an access point to Mount Adams and the Gifford Pinchot National Forest in southwest Washington.

Standing sentinel over Trout Lake is Mt. Adams, the second highest mountain in Washington. Klickitat, its original name, comes from the Chinook word for "beyond." This volcanic cone looms over the farming valley. Canyon scenery along the White Salmon River offers Class II-IV glacial whitewater. One of the United States' first national forests was traced out on the slope of Mt Adams, establishing a legacy of conservation. The forest was named for Gifford Pinchot, the first Chief of the U.S. Forest Service.

Broadfork Farm irrigates with water from the White Salmon River that runs into the Columbia River. Trout Lake sits roughly 53 miles from the Dalles Dam which inundated Celilo Falls where native people fished for centuries. The farm is 21 miles north of the wind-surfing heaven and micro-breweries of Hood River, Oregon. Hikers on the Pacific Crest Trail use Trout Lake as a supply town. There is little traffic through town except when the Fourth of July parade brings out decorated John Deere tractors and politicians throw candy from convertibles.

The farm is less than five miles from the businesses of Trout Lake. There's one convenience-grocery store. The gas station sells burgers, espresso and huckleberry smoothies and hosted my daughter's bridal rehearsal dinner where I wore moth wings as the "motha of the bride." There's a farmer's market, a bar & restaurant and vacation rentals. Closer to the farm is the hardware store whose signboard announces village happenings. A few quick turns down the road is a Zen Buddhist Abbey surrounded by sunflowers.

The Ancient One was laid to rest on tribal lands on February 17, 2017 after a long legal battle with the Smithsonian Museum over his remains.

# The Klickitats

I'm a farmsitter, once or twice a year, a few weeks.
I learned the mountain's name as Mt. Adams, not Klickitat.

Bonneville Dam floods old Celilo Falls. Fireside history
shared before Europeans cut the mountain into rectangles,
when meadow, mountain, salmon, and glacier tingled
under one wind explain how the people learned to weave
water-tight cedar baskets for their berries.
How two volcanoes, Klickitat and Wy'east,
one on each side of the river, fought
over a woman, throwing flames
and molten rock that sizzled into the river.
People came to fish the Celilo narrows,
bury their dead on spirit islands,
meet over and over again for harvests,
trade of goods, huckleberries and salmon.

A surge in white water and urgent winds
bend everything, even tree spirits.
From bedrock, these people knew river mist,
gorge gusts and the mountain's moods
for thousands of years. These people
who walked on, forced away,
who know the rightness
of the bones of Ancient One,
Kennewick Man, coming home.

     I listen.
     Land that holds them
     and feeds me.

"Eating is an agricultural act."
– Wendell Berry

# Buddha Nestled in White and Pink Sweet Peas on the Fencepost at Broadfork Gate

This farm is not for everyman.
In the old house, there's no white sugar,
no microwave and when the first money
slapped down for land, no tractor, just a U-bar
digging fork with as many tines
as a March hare has fancies and that
was how it would be. A broadfork.
Young marrieds moved in with dogs
into a blue-and-magenta striped house
on twenty-two acres of land one local said
was studded with too many scrapes of basalt
to be of much use to anyone, this spot
where pioneers built the first icehouse
on the slopes of Mt. Adams.
The barn needed a new roof
and some jacking back to level.

Not enough land for agri-business,
a farm to feed a few and teach caring,
how to bring good food to a sustainable table.

Husband and wife saw what anyone could see,
the to-die-for view of Mt. Adams,
how an old milking parlor could work
as a classroom for students. On the wall
*"Eating is an agricultural act."* —
Wendell Berry.
Farm-stay students camp in a pasture,
tend kitchen gardens, and care
for pigs, goats, chickens, sheep and ducks.
Tinkerers, menders, reusers, learners,
Buddha and the Broadfork.

# Left with the Wind

The family scurries children, carseats, and luggage
to the airport to go canoeing and camping back East.

As the chain clinks down on the metal fence, we look
at each other and hear deep silence

broken only with dog yawns, grass rustle,
the calls of mourning doves, and the rusty bicycle

sound of chicks in a nursery. A breeze sways
the new orchard of plums and apples,

this quiet which even the sharp contrail
cannot slice through.

# Left with the Care

The banty rooster's strident call
is light years from grinding war, spinning news,
suspicions of sects and warring politicians.
His raucous bluster reminds me of a push-button
toy gargling squawks only a child enjoys.

A hawk whistles across the pasture.
The rooster heard it, a wild away.
He pesters his minions to obey
and the flock does ... to a point.
Broody hens' chicken brains fog
with love for an egg no chick will ever crack.

The rest of the silky bantams
trot their majorette top knots
in proximity but not formation.
A dance I know – take direction
just so; retain waywardness as needed.

My dog flinches from the rooster who flies in her face.
This morning she quivered watching
a deer glean from the apple tree.

Goat squadron commander Mary teaches
about the wildness of goat slit eyes, her kind
who have wandered with people
for nine thousand years.
Her kids butt heads.

The barn cats sneak up in morning mists
that swaddle the valley walls.
The bay mare accepts
hand-offered lush grass, blows at me.

We won't be here very long, gone back
to demagogues, bluffs and bloodshed.
So much singing blues

in the patience of broodiness.
I gather the wariness of goat eyes,
warm wind comfort, cat focus,
the sweetness of ripe pears, mountain fog,
columbine seeds, and dappled eggs.
I may need them all.

# The Flying Saucer

Fear did not bring us out this night, just awe
at another *altocumulus lenticularis*, lens cloud,

cupped like a yarmulke, over the peak.
A convex lens aimed to the heavens

as sunset drenches the mountain
in rose alpenglow. Vapor testimony

to eddied winds, telling downdrafts,
swirls of motions, the mountain's mass,

and yes, we could believe in the presence
of aliens, spirits or those who choose

to witness in the heights of mountains
the felt unidentified, perhaps divine.

# To Tuck In Barnyard Creatures

Ducks at dusk flow into their hutch.
  Their scum-pond stills for tomorrow
  as a latch-gate comes down to save them.

The rooster blocks the door into his henhouse,
  his oily magnificence ready to roil as the door closes
  and the hens push and shuffle up to roosts.

The kittens – soon to be barn cats –
  seek and find fleece on the window ledge.
  A mouse rustles behind kitchen canisters.

The pig gives up on begging squeals
  to bring a rain of sweet grain over the fence
  and trotters away to gilt dreams and rumble-grunts.

The guard dog has dug his hole near the fence,
  rolled in the errant wool the lambs left
  and sniffs leftover feathers of the headless hen.

The yard dog chased two deer from the orchard,
  baby trees of figs, pears and hardy apples.
  She barked once at a gunshot.

All there is left, this starry night of the valley
  with a mountain topped in cloud hats
  is to find my way to a rest as wary as theirs.

# Witnesses

No lament
in the clang of the loose
barn roof in the wind.

No reproof
in the distant flood light,
yellow to the white

of turning stars.
No reminder moon
up early.

Just froideur of stars
among cedars
on a hot summer night.

The silent hens in a row
on rugged perches
see the door closing.

# Checking Fencelines

for Gillian Galford and Dave Trevithick,
Wedding at Broadfork Farm on July 25, 2015

Marriage is hands-on farm management.
Balance books with dreams and sunrises.
Chase piglets that squirm through fences.
Let kittens abide in the hayloft.
Make dogs leave chickens alone.
Collect blue eggs in a wire basket.

Cultivate to reap.
Weed between bean sprouts.
When you hear the creek run,
bless it.

Every day, every week, every month
walk the perimeter of your marriage.
Look inward from the boundary,
seedlings here depend
on the sprawling tree there.
See one big picture
in your album pages.
Savor hedgerows.
Check the fenceline.
Share repairs.

The sun sets on the mountain
at different times each day.
Let love rock you
to sleep.

# Motha of the Bride

I gave her being, this woman with hair of gold.
When her man held out tied fishing flies, a ring in the center,

at that second I became the motha of that bride,
a flitting nuisance at the back porch light

or a graying shade of summer darting at street lamps.
My gray, sultry wings closed against the wind, hunkered.

She dances at the flame of light on diamonds.
I emerge mid-night, open to the flapping of bats.

She dresses in white lace and clutches wild cornflowers,
about to sip the gold wine. I flutter at nectar

discovering at dawn
I am silkworm

who did indeed spin something beautiful.

Poems by Tricia Knoll

# Stars Over the Barn

The physics of twinkling
    stellar scintillation
a river of stars over the black barn
    Milky Way
the flicker of a million million
    a straw thief's escape path of light
on a farm tucked in the valley
    night silence of hens
no better than this.

The turbulence of air
    allows a sunrise
through rib-bone clouds and geese
    so low to the ground
my hair ripples as sunshine
    creeps over the east hills
my shadow is a mile-long
    melt of dew
the cursing world a world away
    never better than this.

# The Mare's Eye

Rest your nervous eye, my blinking beauty.
My hand comes up slow to your nostrils
so you take in the all of me,
the all of me that seeks to nuzzle your cheek,
the whole that knows how we soothe
each other, the soft tips of your ears
turned to consider trust of my low shushes.

I am not predator, and for this moment
you are not herd, not chased, not pushed
to go anywhere except into the quiet
rustle of hay flakes where mice nest
in the straw and the gray barn cat
curls its tail against the sliding door.
You know all of this,
the over and over
how we gentle each other.

Poems by Tricia Knoll

# High Alert and the Night Slinks

The alerts of the guard dog
fracture a glassy night
before moonrise.

His barks echo
off the hills back to base.
The barn motion light

comes on. Is it rats
nibbling downed apples
bucketed for hungry pigs

or that raccoon who lurks nearby
out for duck eggs?
Night is slashed open.

My cone of flashlight
finds reflecting eyes.
Night-prowl cats

follow me, curious
green eyeshines.
Whatever caused

this call to arms
has passed
into dark pasture.

We responders part ways
to settle into sleep
convinced our lights chased

away great evil
so the moon may rise
in silence.

# Hot Night on the Farm

This, every hot night of my life,
screenless windows jaw open
so country crickets saw their songs
without reverb of concrete.

Three police-car moths beeline
to bounce inside the paper lantern shade
though now, after alpenglow turned
the glaciers pink, a latent hope arises

for night winds to melt the fake
starch with which I held onto the day –
a tan line at my socks that proves
I walked eight hot walks

to deliver cold water to cats
and turn on drips for the sapling
filberts and the twiggy apple trees
from France

until I wash my feet for bed,
the rinse of silt testifies to dust.

Poems by Tricia Knoll

# Sun-Up in Late July

A bleached-out moon holds on.
Spike grass inflorescences
light up in gold and nothing suggests
cooler than yesterday, just relief
of early hours as the rooster demands release
to impress his hens and their warm eggs.

Dew sweat on the chain that draws
the tube gate to the fence pole
evaporates while I tricycle to the feed bins
passing chicory the wide color of sky.
At the barn, three cats swirl at my ankles.
Four Canada geese take off from the pond

as if embarrassed to have stopped so long.
The baby chicks' waterer needs refilling
as do the pigs wallowing holes.
Barn swallows on the nest go quiet.
The kittens and the shoats play games

of run and romp with their own kind.
The dogs bury their noses
into ground squirrel holes
and study two teeth-scored apple cores.
I know what's up: 95 by noon.

# Gloucestershire Old Spots

Two steps out of the van, the boldest little girl asks if she can hold a baby pig. I'm not the real farmer, just a stand-in for these neighbor kids, friends. I choose not to answer. (The Old Spots are now darn big even if they are a fifth the size they could grow to be. In this high-nineties heat they have started wallowing in mud instead of dust.)

The chaperones and kids follow me to the barn. The toddler delays at the John Deere toy tractor. I whip out my conversation starter: what do you like about your favorite friends? They say friends should be kind, gentle and fun. I say that's exactly what Gloucestershire Old Spot pigs were bred to be … kind, gentle, friendly to people. Good citizen pigs.

I rattle off that Old Spots are Princess Anne's favorite pigs. Pigs with royal patronage, orchard pigs that can thrive on pasture grass and windfall apples in all kinds of weather. They need shade because they sunburn and can't sweat. I do not mention how factory farms dock pig tails to keep crammed-in neighbors from biting them off. These pigs live the life pigs are meant to live. Nosing for greens, roots and bugs. Loving organic grains. Wallowing. One will live to be a very good mother. The male will be eaten at a neighbor's Christmas Eve.

> hundreds of years
> heritage and breeding
> the perfect small farm pig

Two of these girls visited Broadfork weeks ago when the piglets arrived as timid beings with soft fur. Since then, the farmers and students have nurtured these pigs with chances for petting, clean

---

water, sweet feed and foraging. Gone was soft fur. Added was bulk. No one asked again to pick one up. Everyone petted. We did not talk bacon. This time.

After cursory looks at the meat chicks, lambs, the big white guard dog, and the laying ducks, the adults herded six sweaty and thirsty children back to the van. I wished I'd had time to talk about duck eggs. Next stop inflatable swimming pool, the kid wallow.

That's that. Kids mimicking pig noises. Touching. Barn smells. Hands on. All good.

Then evening. Back to the barn to close the door to the chicken's henitentiary. The lambs had left the barn for pasture to graze in the cool evening wind off the mountain.

I glance into the part of the barn the pigs choose for sleeping. Spooned together in straw against a wall, the two Old Spots snore. I flashback to my tiptoe nights to a crib to check on my infant daughter. Our visitors saw how fast babies grow, how we care for them. How long-time-forever we are wired to love babies, safe and vulnerable in sleep.

# The Sign to Dream Café

*"The plane don't leave 'til midnight –*
*come with me today.*
*They'll be plenty of time to be alone,*
*at The Dream Cafe."*
*– Greg Brown*

Above the nailed-up cow skull, in the center of the multi-forks
of a sprawling sycamore, the sign tilts upward, and two ropes
offer climbers an assist to a safe perch.

This tree is the hub of Broadfork, a refuge
where children find a hammock, two swings, a pillowed bench,
welcome shade the size of a croquet field on a July day.

The bronze sculpture of the roots of another sycamore tree
stands at Ground Zero in New York, a memory
of the ravaged sycamore that saved the windows at St. Paul's

from what fell from the Trade Center. Two anchors.
Humans invest hope in spirit as vigorous
as plane trees, sanctuary from burning,

and roots that go deep.

# Rock and Root

Stone and bone are neat rhymes,
spine and ribcage words
that underpin the path forward.

What of rock and root,
I ask when we walk
the simplest route around
the marsh of old Trout Lake.

An improbable lodgepole pine
leans uphill over the sluggish river cut,
clutches in its thigh roots a rock
as thick as a goat. That stone tumbled

in mudslides the volcano let loose
eons ago.  Twisted, rugged root tissue
cradles precious rock eggs.
Roots and boulders here

twist up like satisfied lovers
legs over torsos, arms about necks.
We, on our stonework stroll,
admire the cut-away

where the river did
its work.

# The Night of the Salmon-Go-Up-River Full Moon

A full moon blesses this cooling-off
July night, the farm, the black currants,
the tin-roof barn, the Old Spot pigs.

You and I snuggle under a comforter
as the willow sways in eddied wind.
Bone-white light stretches long javelins

of moonshine from the ten-window door,
ladders of light we don't choose to climb
this time, a silver hopscotch on the oak floor.

Brighter than street light by my measure.
I could walk to the barn, swing
in the Nicaraguan hammock. By moon.

Your breathing deepens, a whuffing
under flutter wind. The white dog
barked at a hawk earlier; now he curls

in gold grass. Wads of his fur that I brushed out
this morning mix with the wild yarrow
and cling to fence wire, fluff ghosts.

Mt. Adams' south rib glacier gleams.
I am alive to unwavering moonlight,
warmed up in a soft bed

seeing the world
as a negative image, both black
and white night,

foreshadow of memory.

## "Every menu is an obituary."

### – Wislawa Szymborska

The carrot pulled from the soil
goes as limp as the dead chicken.
Both become my body.

Our incisors and canines, jawbones
are made for meat. Methane-cloud debates
spark a burn for those who starve
or exclude flesh from dinner.

This farm place
small-scale organic, participant
food for locavores, neither fast
    (patience for swelling butternuts)
nor so very slow
    (weeks for the gold-red chickens)
abundance of eggs.

This family table
where each knows
the life they swallow.
We fed them, led them
from pasture to barn.
Watered. Worried.
Patted and pressed.
Death remains
bound for compost piles
to feed the worms
that go to growing.

Poems by Tricia Knoll

The sale of extra.
The best that can be done
within the circle
of impermanence.
Hope as maintenance.

# The Farmer Hides in a Tree

A place he wasn't supposed to be, near a blast zone,
nearly a hundred years after the fact, the Condit Dam
on the White Salmon River was dynamiting
down and he wanted to see. Concrete that
stopped salmon from coming upriver,
glacial melt that irrigated his property.
Hiding in a tree to see a breaching,
free-flow returned to a wild river
he hears each night. Thirty-three
miles of spawning ground
reconnected. A new course
for water and his children.

Condit Dam, an impoundment completed in 1913, was intentionally
breached on October 26, 2011. On that date it was the largest
dam ever removed in the United States.

Poems by Tricia Knoll

# Untended Pasture

No hoof prints. Fallow, fenced
for steers, or milk goats that scamper
volcanic rock piles. Wild sweet peas,

lupine, and seeds stalks of pasture grass
reel in wind off the mountain, respond like crowds
to a touchdown to stand, sway.

Mullein, waist-high
stiff stalk, thrives to bed
in unwatered holdings,

towers above the furry rosette
in a second season.
I am this mullein

in forgotten places
where my yellow flowers
come on few enough

to keep me straight,
and one or two
beautiful.

# To the Diarist on the Maine Farm, 1947

*for Henry Beston*

I was being born in a big city, what you call
the idiot world of vitamin pills.
The train couldn't go fast enough
to bring you back to your iced-over pond
that moans, a welcome fire kindled in your stove.

Would I trade for your world, your winter
kitchen with the painting of two draft horses
pulling a fire wagon, horses you named Prince and Major
for your neighbor's white plough horses who till
your fields for corn, harvest hay. Your wheeled year
of spring's mud ruts, fall's smell of rotting apples.
One in five people were farmers then, now one in fifty.
Your people of color are bare-chested neighbors
you lovingly call Indians, sun-tanned from the fields.

I envy how you listen. Your cistern fills.
Bobolinks. Jays. A rooster. And what you knew.
Why the pig ailed. When alewives run.
The route the swallows take south
in fall. The practicality of a chopping block
of locust wood. You read to your wife
while she darns socks, feel for young men
just home from war. Rain's one worry.
Your neighbor's hay, the corn. Another the brush
of a new pesticide on your skin. Hold your reveries
on smoke from chimneys across the pond, whether
fireflies light for love or whimsy. You loved
summer yard sales on old Route 1, displays
for out-of-state plates of hooked rugs, toy lobster pots,
coon kittens, and doughnuts in a crock.

Before Targets, Walmarts. Our unending wars.
We agree on a name for what remains
of uncut woods, The Enchanted.
How we go in deep to feel
what the earth needs. Lingering
footprints of wild –
snowshoe hare, fox, the moose
and the returned wolf loping
under the Big Dipper
you call The Plough.

# Lifting The Irrigation Valves

A keep-green-growing walk from spigot to spigot,
a handle on the hydrant valve for the rain bird
swivel, click and click and click, how it goes.

Three birds grab the hot day. Two hawks
circle-kettle over the henhouse
to see blue-and-green-egg hens.

The bald eagle north to south
over two Freedom meat chickens
that escaped the fencing.

The eagle's straight line
as if threading a needle to stab
the sun of a perfect day.

# Death of the Sussex Rooster

He's not a stew; our dog did it.
Grabbed him, opened his gut,
ate his left leg and dropped
his brilliance of black, white and red
feathers and glistening guts at my feet.

No more crowing
to dawn, no wake up,
just motley orange and white hens
at the henitentiary door waiting
a day in too much heat.

My sleepless night under stars
stirred guilt soup. This one chicken
stands inside my hard hangover
of those who kill.
We should have known.

The golden lab
dug him up from his burial
in the pasture, ran home
high proud with zombie chicken.
This could have been avoided.

# September

A dry gorge wind-blast spreads wildfires
that twist the mountain silver and haze the sky,
sends a black dog to hide in tractor tire shadows
to keep one eye on ground squirrels in the rock piles.

The kittens that tore the mourning dove in half
under stabs of starlight day-rest on cool concrete
of a barn floor. The pig begs for rotten apples
and deformed pears. Eight brown ducks slide

from hutch to pond, an orderly school.
I consider kale for dinner and hope
the clothespins keep the linens on the line.
New barn metal clatters and spins a song

to the old wood barn standing stolid.
We, you and me, barely speak
as the wind shows how leaves
that tumble do skitter like mice.

# The Washington State Heritage Barn

Farm bones, its crib, the rest stop
for a century's parade of cows, horses, goats,
sheep, chickens, cats, dogs, children,
and farmers that hold tight
to the worn-downs of their lives.

A leaky frame sieves bust-up winds
and download snows, ghost filters.
Inches of dry manure and straw
earth down to piles of scuffled gold.
Stanchions witness to the neck-rubbing
of grazers reaching for hay. Pocket nests
of barn swallows blend into weathered beams.
A place of spit, pee, head butts and mouse poop.
Hideout from drought and long-day heat.
The curl of a kitten's tail against my feet.
Mary, the queen goat's brazen eyes.
The symphony groans of metal and fir.
Three cotton sling chairs hung
from the rafters for a nursing mother,
ruts below where feet push off from sawdust.

Scribbles of calculations on old wood,
a faded phone number. Built north to south
to catch the most sun, a ray breaks
through the gap in the hayloft.
Where history sits squarely
or not so squarely
on retrofitted foundations.

# The Lingua Franca of Huckleberries

The eyes of the supreme spirit fell
onto the high plateau around Klickitat
and rooted out in runners
into the heaven fields of meadow,
forest and lakes as huckleberries.

Drying the berries for winter
brought fires, games, horse races,
time for tanning hides. The best
fields wait for first people's picking.

Down in the valley tart/sweet
smoothies mix up huckleberries
at the gas station and diner
where bicycle riders
and Harleys stop by. Those pies.
The feast the tongue knows.

# The Chubby Buddhist Monk of Trout Lake Abbey

His abbey sits in fields of echinacea and lavender
beyond the llama pasture, surrounded in sunflowers.
The summer winds stir a dozen temple bells.

He wears robes of brown and melon orange,
grows huge *helianthus*, nurtures barn bats, tends
a garden of one hundred Buddhas.

Kozen, the man, trains his rollicking mutts.
He stopped in the small town across the Columbia
to let them sniff and express dog-nature

when a man assaulted him screaming epithets
against Muslims, cut his face, kicked his car door
and fled. A hate crime on the police sheet.

Kozen to the TV camera: *You are completely forgiven.*
*The Buddha tells us all of our suffering*
*comes from anger, desire and ignorance.*

At home, prayer wheels and wind chimes
play in limbs of trees near the end of their time.
Long grasses in the mountain's breath.

# Gray Hope

I fold back our bed sheets this morning
to match the rolls of cloud billows
sliding like pillows into the naked hot sky.

My feet slip to the tuck at the mattress
to test the cool slickness that may be rain
on a horizon of gray hope

this drought might end.

# A Bite Out of Drought

Last night gorge wind blustered down and shook the barn,
frantic wind to follow up weeks of droughted summer.

Crunchy hard fall pears, some call them winter pears, plunked
down into gold grass. We still hoped wind brought rain.

We got mist. Floaty fog, a sky-lifting mid-morning
curtain opening on foothills but not Klickitat. Gauziness

without water. The golden lab grabbed a knocked-down
tennis ball-green pear, tossed it as if it might bounce.

She took bites, one, then another and another,
one bite per fruit, the pears I'd hoped to poach.

Those pears with white, oxidizing-brown bites,
gouges the shape of fallen angels.

# Good for an October Day

A bruised apple
and the last onions
wrapped in tight skin,
to the soup pot.

Once field fires
smoldered
for ghosts to decide
what they made of themselves
in the burn-aroma of leaves.

Overlooked windfall pears
only good for a day
or maybe two.

# A Blessing Over Fruit

Late October is past ripeness. Where we walk,
the dog and I, we see the fallen figs,
Italian plums flat like dead bats,
dried up canes of raspberries.
Windfall apples dotted with spots
of coddling moth worms.

My dog does not acknowledge end. She reaches
for dried-out blackberry husks with mold.
She grabs a mouthful of salal berries
as if jammed in her teeth they might taste like jelly.

I eat red grapes, drool over peaches
and gush red plums from the new orchard
in their time. I try to tell her
we have had this blessing.
We have moved on.
All will be well,
we will be fed, she may find joy in a snowball.

She has a very flamboyant tail, this farm dog,
and she ignores my advice, a flag-waving fool.
Her nose seeks hard-green kiwis, persimmons
that await first frosts to ripen.

I kick scarlet, yellow and orange leaves
as though they are gold candles,
sheriff's badges and tangerine peels.

# Guardians

Spying Canada geese stray from the wildlife refuge.
There's forgiving eyes of She Who Watches down the river,

a metal chinook swinging on the entry gate,
the sloop that sails on the weather vane,

Buddha and his beads, in the stillness
as a farm rests, the after-noon siesta

amid the slow swelling of green grapes,
a warding peace nestles inside and around.

When night cracks open in staccato barks,
as sleep yielded responsibility

to the big white dog
in the back field – alert reader

of wind, rustles and wingbeats,
we are grateful to what watches over.

# Farmku

silence
down the farm road
ice locks the mailbox

first light
dew on the fence chain
and mourning doves

leaking hoses
wrapped in duct-tape
in a pinch

bone-white full moon
through the windowed door
a break with the past

sun so bright
my laptop screen
mirrors peace

tattered paper parasol
on the table saw
last year's wedding

the mini-tool bench
the boy is losing teeth
and cutting boards

happy birthday card
from the hardware store
farmer's nuts, bolts, and hoses

barn cats
play the cool dawn
thundering feet

catcalling
and back pedaling
the season of stone fruits

returning an overlooked
full-body mirror
that shared past

the scarecrow
drops her bra
in the forget-me-nots

dogs sleep
in rug shadows
of the laundry line

a sturdy fence,
loved land
and homegrown corn

wistful going home
after farm stay
my goat voice

Poems by Tricia Knoll

# Coming Down the Mountain in Mid-November to the Farm

I praise first light that silvers the first snow
on white pines. A two-inch burden on the hood
and roof of my Volvo, what we never saw coming
as night came on. I praise the haste I know
to take, revving the car down valley to the farm,
my caution skirting bath-size mud puddles
in the gravel road. Parking beyond the gate,
so Bear, the Great Pyrenees, can't escape,
I slip my body in with my hands full
as his barks bounce off metal gate rails.
He seems to have doubled in size, a winter
undercoat ballooned since summer.

He prances me past the apple tree starts,
the gazebo for the woodstove logs,
through randomness of fallen sycamore leaves
to the two children in their quilted suits
and striped wool hats. Fisher's milk teeth,
blue eyes and pink cheeks. The gap
between Rye's two new teeth. I praise
their smiles as I hand them the first snowballs
from up the mountain. How quickly they eat
the melting balls. I praise impermanence.

Prompted by his father, Rye tells of seeing
a black bear at the Bonneville fish hatchery.
The guard dog stands at my side
as my fingers, bright red from carrying slush,
burrow into his fur weathering
into the color of old snow.

I praise abundance.

# An Uncommon Prayer for the Farm

## after Brian Doyle

This morning three cracked and cleaned-out ducks eggs rested in mud. The ducks fail to understand the laying-egg purpose of the coop they share with broody hens. Some egg eater tasted the night under Bear's radar.

*First petition: safety.*

Yellow jackets nest in the propane tank lid. A dead squirrel showed up yesterday in the grass while innocent-acting dogs begged for a romp down to the creek. A mother tiger-cat stepped aside to let her kitten finish off a garter snake, her hand-me-down hunting dance. Later she ate a mouse. Two hawks flew in concentric rings over the chicken yard until Bear barked. I move in slow motion to get five range-born lambs to accept grain from my hand. Fated to become chops and roasts, they have a right to be skittish.

*May we be safe within the confines of our being.*

A farm is always in want of something. The deep hole we dug to the cracked irrigation valve needed filling. That's where we buried the squirrel. The piglets had metal tags in their ears before they came here to fatten up into proud Gloucestershire Old Spot pigs. One ear oozed the day before yesterday. Then the ear crusted up. Now the tag is gone. A praying mantis rides around on my hair barrette.

*So: repair. Heal what can be healed.*

Today – clear sky summer and a grass tickle-breeze. Willa, black herding dog, pants in sycamore shade. The kittens made a straw nest in the goat barn. Three species of butterflies are out and about, as are the moths that head-banged the lamps the other night. Black currants, blueberries and raspberries are ripe. Organic vegetables are swelling up, and sure, abundant kale, and the first cucumber.

*Repair of gratitude. Life – the circle we seek to see.*

# Refracted Light

Come to the end, hook to clasp, as at the beginning,
I smell maple bacon, lines in bacon striped fat and lean,
imagine left to write as an ant's obsession to follow
the smell of trail. The mountain hovers like a picture
I could pencil on a postcard. Two dogs wiggle for kibble,
and the guardian gets his inner ears cleaned. One of those hens
is laying another blue egg. Two hawks again circle over
the henhouse. A dozen dozen swallows balance on
the electric wires end to end, mandala beads of my counting.
A teardrop crystal cracks open morning's light
into jigging rainbows on the kitchen's rag rug,
while bees bump at the window glass,
bees that humble-bumble one bloom to the next.

# Acknowledgments

Grateful acknowledgment is made to the editors of the following publications in which these poems first appeared:

*Cirque – A Literary Journal for the North Pacific Rim*, "Witnesses"

*Defy!* (an anthology from Robocup Press), "The Chubby Buddhist Monk of Trout Lake Abbey"

*Poetry Breakfast*, "Checking Fencelines"

*Plum Tree Tavern*, "Gray Hope" and "A Bite Out of Drought"

*Verse-Virtual*, "The Sign to Dream Café," "The Flying Saucer" and "To the Diarist on the Maine Farm, 1947"

*Verseweavers*, "Root and Rock"

*Visitant*, "An Uncommon Prayer for the Farm"

*Windfall – A Journal of Poetry of Place*, "To Tuck in Barnyard Creatures"

# Praise for Broadfork Farm

At a glance, *Broadfork Farm* might seem a rustic homage to a simpler sort of life — and it is that — but the poems are rich with energies, convergences with and retreats from our cultural moment. Subtly, the poems ask to engage with the realities of the farm — the violences of barnyard cats and dogs, the slaughter of lambs, the impact of a long drought — and to hold these in comparison and contrast with the banal forces of history: the brutal conquests of Native lands, terror attacks at home and abroad, a hate crime against a Buddhist monk "mistaken" for a Muslim.

Knoll is a skilled poet; "To Tuck in Barnyard Creatures" is one of many poems with a rich sonic texture that is both subtle and celebratory — sometimes it feels as if we're in the music of the farm, the songs of the roosters, the barking of the dogs, the rhythms of a different life. By the end of the book, we are asked, perhaps, not only to see and hear "life on the farm" but to see and hear our own lives a little differently. To put it more simply, like its namesake, the poetry of *Broadfork Farm* will "feed a few and teach caring" — and that's a tremendous accomplishment for a book of poems.

Tod Marshall,
Washington State Poet Laureate

For Tricia Knoll, writing poems is a way of participating in the everyday of what matters. While *Broadfork Farm* traces Knoll's experiences in the daily business and busyness at the eponymous farm, her articulate and carefully observant poems simultaneously present evidence of her deep ecological concerns and her compassionate embrace of our world and its human and nonhuman inhabitants. Open this book anywhere and feel the "rustles and wingbeats" of the wind on the farm, as well as Knoll's abundant gratitude for "what watches over."

Andrea Hollander,
Author of *Landscape with Female Figure: New & Selected Poems, 1982 – 2012*

To read Tricia Knoll's *Broadfork Farm* is to come to a gate and find that it opens for you. These aren't poems that stand and talk stiffly at the threshold; these are poems that welcome you into the farm and barn and pastures, poems that walk and work, that see, taste, and listen to this particular loved place. Knoll's poems inhabit the farm as vividly as the community of humans, spotted pigs, broody chickens, goats, and dogs that live there. They roost and burrow and take root. I find myself not so much reading these poems as sticking my head into each one like a bee in a flower, eager to see what is inside. I want to stay a long time in this book's marvelous pasture.

Annie Lighthart,
Author of *Iron String*

# About the Author

Tricia Knoll is an Oregon poet. To her, the Columbia River Gorge is one of the great wonders of the world. She loves crossing the bridge at Hood River, Oregon and heading north to Trout Lake, to Broadfork Farm. For many years, some of her best friends have been creatures with fur or more than two feet.

Her education focused on literature – degrees from Stanford University (B.A.) and Yale University (M.A.T.) She has taught high school English, edited a newspaper for school-age children, worked as the Public Relations Director at Portland's Children Museum, and retired as the Public Information Officer at the Portland Water Bureau. She kept poems on scraps of paper in a drawer.

Her first day of retirement began with walking a dog and sitting to reread Whitman's *Leaves of Grass*. That re-ignited her lifelong love of writing and reading poetry. She maintains a daily haiku writing practice and sometimes calls herself an eco-poet. Her poetry appears widely in national and international journals and anthologies.

Her chapbook *Urban Wild* (Finishing Line Press, 2014) explores interactions between humans and wildlife in urban habitat.

*Ocean's Laughter* (Aldrich Press, 2016) takes its title from a line in Pablo Neruda's *The Book of Questions*: Do you not also fear the sea's laughter? Poetry in *Ocean's Laughter* focuses on change over time in Manzanita, a small town on Oregon's north coast.

Knoll is extremely grateful for the poet-mentors she has studied with and her poet-friends who continue to inspire and encourage her.

Website: triciaknoll.com

Twitter: @triciaknollwind

# About The Poetry Box

The Poetry Box® was founded in 2011 by Shawn Aveningo & Robert R. Sanders, who wholeheartedly believe that every day spent with the people you love, doing what you love, is a moment in life worth cherishing. Their boutique press celebrates the talents of their fellow artisans and writers through professional book design and publishing of individual collections, as well as their flagship literary journal, *The Poeming Pigeon*.

Feel free to visit The Poetry Box® online bookstore, where you'll find more books including:

*Keeping It Weird: Poems & Stories of Portland, Oregon*

*The Way a Woman Knows* by Carolyn Martin

*Of Course, I'm a Feminist!* edited by Ellen Goldberg

*Giving Ground* by Lynn M. Knapp

*Poeming Pigeons: Poems about Birds*

*The Poeming Pigeon: Poems about Food*

*The Poeming Pigeon: Doobie or Not Doobie?*

*The Poeming Pigeon: Poems about Music*

*The Poeming Pigeon: Poems from the Garden*

*and more ...*

# Order Form

Need more copies for friends and family?  No problem. We've got you covered with two convenient ways to order:

1. Go to our website at www.thePoetryBox.com, click on Bookstore.

    or

2. Fill out the order form. Email it to Shawn@thePoetryBox.com

    (Bookstores can order via Ingram or email Shawn)

Name: _____

Shipping Address: _____

_____

Phone Number:  (____) _____

Email Address: _____@_____

Payment:  __Cash  __Check  __PayPal Invoice  __Credit Card

Credit Card #: _____ CCV _____

Expiration Date:_____Signature:_____

*Broadfork Farm* by Tricia Knoll

# of Copies: _____

x $12.00: _____

Plus Shipping & Handling:  $3.50

Order Total: _____

## Thank You!

CPSIA information can be obtained
at www.ICGtesting.com
Printed in the USA
FSOW04n0526040717
35925FS